ADULT COLORING BOOKS

FLORAL

MANDALA PATTERNS

Vol.3

STRESS RELIEVING ART THERAPY

FOR BUSY PEOPLE

COLOR TEST PAGE

COLOR TEST PAGE

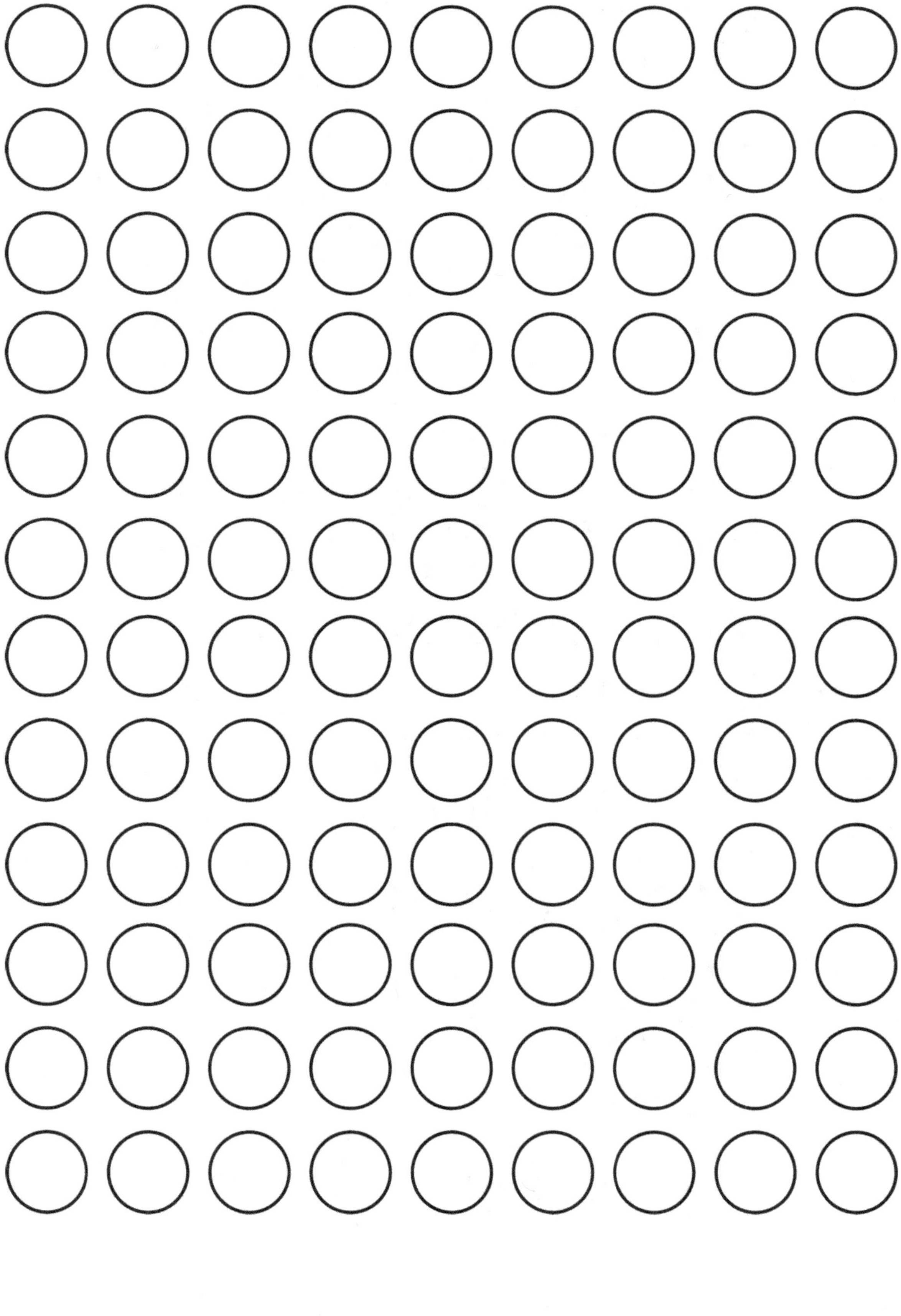

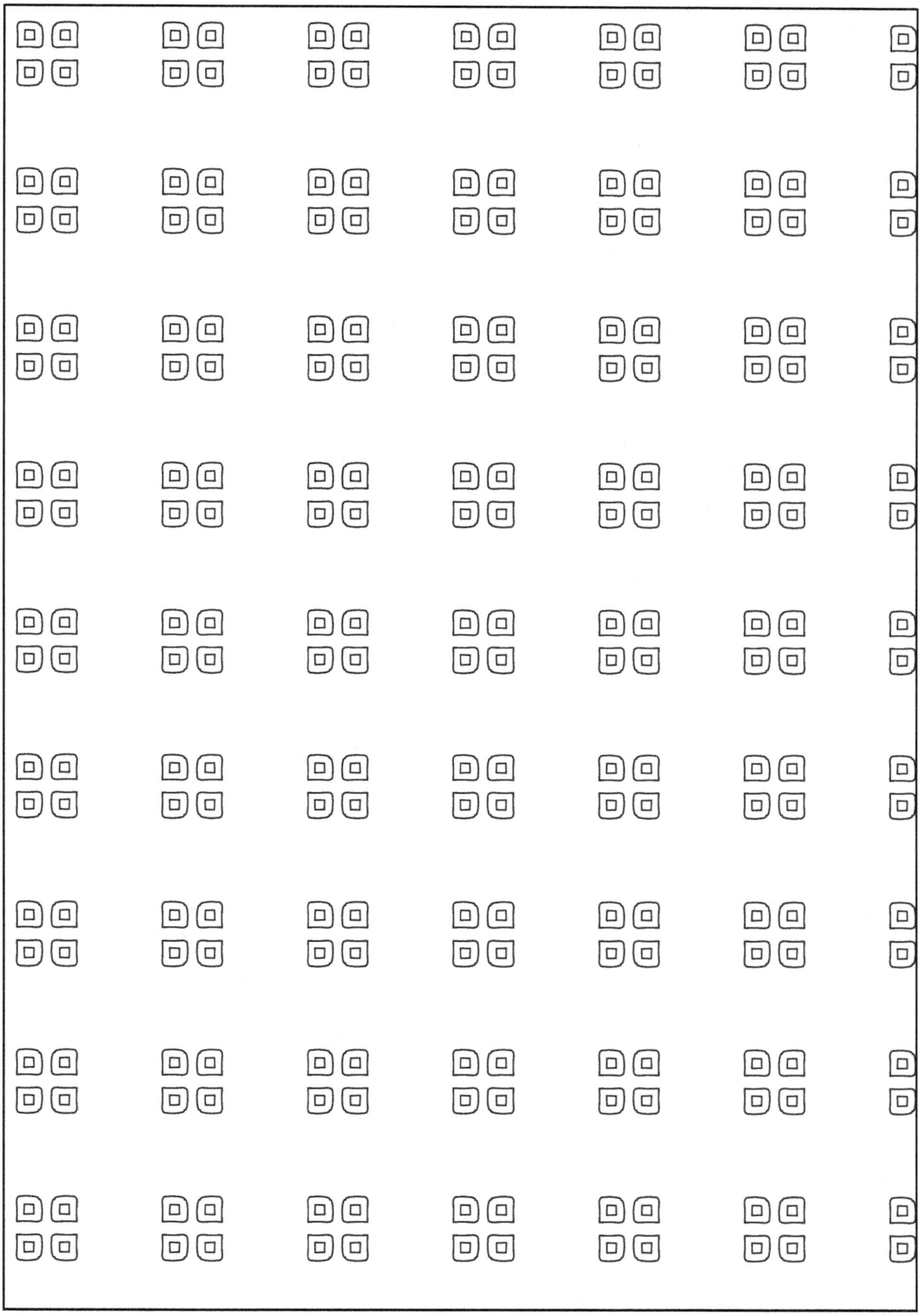

www.ingramcontent.com/pod-product-compliance
Lightning Source LLC
Chambersburg PA
CBHW081856280526
45789CB00007B/2720
9781537696652